HOME MADE WINES

from
Lorraine & Ian

3 . 1 . 1974

HOME-MADE WINES

HOW TO MAKE THEM

BY

PEGGY HUTCHINSON

AND

MARY WOODMAN

LONDON

W. FOULSHAM & CO. LTD.

NEW YORK   TORONTO   CAPETOWN   SYDNEY

W. FOULSHAM & CO. LTD.
Yeovil Road, Slough, Bucks, England

ISBN 0 - 572 - 00182 - 7

MADE IN GREAT BRITAIN BY
John Gardner (Printers) Ltd.
Liverpool 20

CONTENTS

INTRODUCTION

A great number of people associate home-made wine with rather old-fashioned maiden aunts who bring out tiny glasses of very sweet home-made parsnip wine, one sip of which sends the vicar reeling away on his rounds of parish calls.

Well, until recent years, the only people who still made wine at home were countrywomen who had grown up with a wine-making tradition, and it may well be that they preferred the strong sweet wines rather than the drier table wines.

Although home-made wines carry the distinctive flavours of the fruit or other ingredients from which they are made, they can mostly be varied from sweet to dry, according to your taste. You can have a sparkling or a still table wine, as dry as the driest hock, or a rich sweet dessert wine. A good home-made grape wine could equal some of the best that was ever imported into this country: even if not exceptional, it is usually better than a great number of run-of-the-mill table wines on the market today. Bonuses include the fact that many home-made wines have a definite affinity for certain foods. Apricot wine is delectable with fish, and orange wine without parallel with roast duck or goose. Gooseberry wine is virtually indistinguishable from champagne.

Wine-making is a fascinating hobby. The equipment is inexpensive, and much of it can be found in every home. Nor is wine-making difficult. A certain amount of care, and a few reasonable precautions, need to be taken.

Wine-making is no longer a purely country pursuit, but it does need more room than is available in, say, a modern flat kitchenette, simply because the wine must stand for a few months without being moved, and, in a confined space, it would get in the way. A dry shed, outhouse or a garage, failing a special 'still-room', is quite adequate, and if you adopt the hobby with any sort of seriousness, it is well worth investing in a small shed for the purpose, because your wine will work out at about a shilling a bottle, and you'll save yourself a lot of money.

But you mustn't sell it. You may legally make as much as you like for yourself and your family and guests, but you musn't sell a drop of it, or even give it to be sold at the Church bazaar, without an excise licence. Whatever you do, you must not attempt to distill it. Apart from being strictly illegal, this is an extremely dangerous pastime.

Home-made wines are far from being fruit juices with a slight kick, and in many cases the alcoholic content can exceed that of bought wines. Wine is made to be enjoyed, and complete enjoyment presupposes moderation. If in the excitement of sampling your first vintage, (after a wait of about twelve months), you get carried away, we offer the following sovereign remedies to make the head feel smaller:

1. Be wise before the event. Take a dessert-spoon of milk of magnesia or a teaspoon of olive oil before you start heavy drinking.

2. Avoiding the 'hair of the dog', which simply piles misery upon misery, try one of the following:

(a) A prairie oyster, which is a whole raw egg with Worcester Sauce, downed quickly, which is, after all, the only way to get it down.

(b) Your chemist will give you his own remedy for a hob-nailed liver, and probably grin nastily as he makes it up.

(c) If you can bear it, drink cold milk before going to bed, and take Alka-Seltzer or Eno's in the morning, followed at eleven by a drink of Fernet-Branca, a very effective but vile-tasting Italian drink, nasty enough to serve as a warning as well as a cure.

The writer Francoise Sagan advocated vanilla ice-cream for breakfast as a cure for over-indulgence, but most people would rather keep the hangover.

There are, of course, hundreds of recipes for home-made wines, and in this book we give a few of the 'standards'. Compiling your own recipe book is one of the interesting side-lights of this engrossing hobby. A few evenings at the public library will yield recipes by the score, and many old recipe books, such as Mrs. Beeton's, can often tell you how to make some of the more unusual types of wine, possibly not mentioned in our recent wine-making books. When you are in the country, you can some-times find people who have family recipes, often of incredible antiquity, the possession of these can give you a very special kind of 'Wineupmanship'.

It is not always possible to taste someone else's brew before you make a particular type of wine, so it is better to make small quantities at first, until you find out what wines are to your taste. If your wine disappoints you because you find it too dry or too sweet, alter the recipe slightly by using more or less sugar, until the result is more to your liking. All recipes originated from individuals, who may have preferred a wine drier or sweeter than you care about.

If your first attempts at wine making are not an outstanding success, don't give it up as a bad job, or write yourself off as an unlucky wine maker. Luck doesn't enter into it. In the course of reading this book, you will learn what the pitfalls are, and if you fall into one of them, you will simply have to be more careful next time. It is very disappointing to wait six months or more to taste your first wine, and then find that something has gone wrong with it. You will probably have neglected some small point, and extra care with the next batch is sure to remedy the matter.

You can make wine in every month of the year, if you like. After the soft fruit season is over, October brings cider apples, November celery and marrow. Seville oranges are plentiful and cheap in January, and raisins, dates, figs, ginger and dried apricots are available almost all the year round. Some flowers also make excellent wine in season.

You can establish a rotation plan, not only in your wine-making, but in the seasons in which it will be ready to drink. Orange wine made in January is ready for the following Christmas. March's ginger wine will warm the cockles of your heart throughout the following winter.

Always label your bottles as soon as they are corked, and add the earliest date on which it can be broached. Wines in the bottle look very much alike, and it would be a pity to open the wrong one by mistake, because once opened, it must be drunk within a reasonably short time, and it may not be ready or, worse still, it may be something you intended to save for a grand occasion.

You will have vintage years, just as vignerons all over the world do. This is not to say that your wines will vary a great deal, because they won't, but vintage years are a wonderful bonus, a rare happening, and one of the joys of wine-making.

When you have six or eight different wines in your 'cellar' with perhaps a plentiful supply of cider or whatever wine you prefer as your *vin ordinaire*, and one or two bottles of something rather special, you are in a position comparable to that of a very rich man. You can say, as few people can say, "I think I'll have a glass of such-and-such", and go and get it, the sweet, the dry, the red, the white, the still or sparkling, as the fancy of the moment dictates.

And that moment is worth all the trouble you have taken, the care with which you have chosen your ingredients, the preparation of the must, the watching over the fermentation, the racking, the fining and bottling, the waiting for maturity.

A glass of wine always offers you something special, but never as special as when you lift your glass to look at the magnificent colour, to smell the fragant bouquet, to taste the delicious wine you have made yourself.

And when better wine is made, if wine can be better than the best we have yet seen, you may very well be the one to make it.

CHAPTER 1

Equipment

A certain amount of equipment is needed in wine-making, and much of it can be found in any household. Whether you want to use this equipment, or keep special utensils for wine-making, is entirely up to you, but it will have to be specially cleaned every time you use it, in any case.

Wine-making equipment should be made of glass, non-resinous wood (preferably oak, beech or ash), earthenware, or polythene. Some metals can be used safely, but with others the acidity of the fruit can cause a chemical reaction which may spoil the wine, or even make it poisonous. The choice of non-metallic con-

15

tainers is so wide you should have no difficulty in gathering them together.

You will need:
1. A wooden chopping or bread board.

2. A sharp stainless steel or silver knife.

3. An enamel or polythene colander.

4. Measuring jugs, a graduated measure, and possibly a set of weighing scales.

5. A large earthenware crock, (or a plastic dustbin as a substitute).

6. A large jug. (The jug from an old-fashioned bedroom jug-and-basin set is ideal).

7. A large jar or small cask.

8. An air-lock.

 9. Four feet of clean rubber or polythene tubing, $\frac{1}{4}$ inch in diameter.

 10. Bottles.

 11. Corks or stoppers.

 12. A wide-necked polythene funnel.

 13. A preserving pan.

 14. Old linen cloth and polythene sheeting.

Jars and Casks

Casks are far better than jars, but unfortunately the days when you could buy them for a couple of shillings are past, and they can be very expensive. There are several advantages to using a cask, because they are designed specifically for wine-making, have a bung at the top that allows the wine to 'breathe' if not knocked home too tightly, and a spigot at the bottom, so that the wine can be drawn off during racking without disturbing the lees. Never use a cask that has been used for anything but wine, *especially* a vinegar cask.

A pleasant way of acquiring a small cask is to persuade someone to give you a little cask of sherry for Christmas. Drink the sherry, and use the cask for ever afterwards for your own wine-making, and your wine will acquire added taste from the sherry. Jars, however, are quite adequate, and are better when made of clear glass.

If there is no shop near you that specialises in wine-making equipment (and a quick look in the local classified telephone directory will tell you), buy or order from any branch of

Boots or Heath & Heather, or from R. Loftus, 24 Tottenham Court Road, W.1. The size of your jar will vary with the amount of wine you intend to make, the smallest economical size being a one-gallon demi-john, although they range right up to twelve gallon carboys.

Better than a plain jar is an aspirator, which has a tap near the base, so that clear wine can be drawn off during racking, leaving the sediment undisturbed.

Your local publican may be able to help you, but with a little imagination you can soon acquire a suitable range of vessels for brewing, and storing.

Air Locks

An air-lock is a simple piece of apparatus, reminiscent of chemistry lessons at school. There are three types in general use, designed to allow gas to escape during fermentation without the introduction of air which could contaminate the brew. This is done by keeping a small volume of water between the fermenting wine and the outside air.

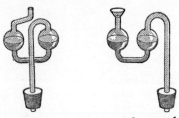

The best air-lock is the manufactured variety, which costs only a few shillings, and is generally used with narrow-necked vessels. This consists of a piece of bent glass tubing with two bulbs blown in it which should be half filled with water.

If a commercial air-lock is not available it is a simple affair to apply the same principle with plastic or rubber tubing.

When fermenting in wide-necked vessels, such as an earthenware crock or a plastic bucket, cover them with a sheet of polythene, or several thicknesses of blanket, and secure with elastic.

Bottles

The type of bottle used will depend on the kind of wine you intend to make. Thick, heavy bottles are needed for sweet or sparkling wines, i.e. champagne bottles or, at a pinch, beer bottles with screw tops. Dry white wines are better in a lighter type of bottle. Red wines need coloured bottles, green or brown, or they will lose colour.

Corks

Straight-sided corks are best, and are not difficult to insert. You can buy a simple corking machine (33/- from Boots), for the purpose, or simply tap them home with a mallet.

Always use new corks. It is impossible to clean old corks, and they rot and crumble rather easily. New corks cost about 1d. each. A small tip when corking bottles: soak the corks for a minute or two in tepid water.

Wires

If you plan to make sparkling wines, it is advisable to wire corks into position. Brewers' sundriesmen supply the correct preformed loops, which save a lot of trouble.

Cloths

These are needed for straining fruit juice, and must be fairly thick, closely woven, and non-fluffy. Old but sound linen sheeting is very good, so is nylon or terylene.

Note: All your wine-making equipment can be bought at Boots, (the Regent Street branch specialises in wine-making requirements), at Heath & Heather, or from W. & R. Loftus and Co., 24 Tottenham Court Road, London, W.1. Most branches of the first two firms will order your requirements for you, if they don't actually stock them, and are very helpful in giving advice. All three companies supply price lists on request, and sell simple wine-making kits for beginners.

Sterilization of Equipment

Make the cleaning and sterilization of all your equipment routine. Growths of undetectable mould will ruin your wine, and your temper.

Your equipment and bottles must be stored in a clean, dry place. If an outhouse or shed is used for storage, a coat of whitewash on walls and ceiling is a great help.

Sterilization procedures are as follows:

1. *Jars*

When storing jars, fill with a solution made from six Campden tablets, (potassium metabisulphite), and a half-ounce of citric acid to a gallon of water. When the jar is to be used, pour away the solution and rinse well, filling right up with water at each rinsing.

2. *Casks*

(a) *New casks.* Fill with a solution of $\frac{1}{4}$ lb. washing soda to a gallon of boiling water. Bung down and leave for 24 hours, then drain and wash thoroughly. Pour in a pint of wine or cider, or a solution of half-ounce citric acid to a gallon of water. Swirl the liquid all round the barrel for half an hour, drain and wash thoroughly. If you neglect to do this, your wine will have a 'woody' flavour.

(b) *Used casks.* If freshly emptied of port, sherry, rum, brandy etc., casks need not be treated, and your wine will carry the extra flavour of its previous contents, which is highly desirable, but the cask must be rinsed.

You can also sterilize all casks, new or old, as follows:

i   Steam the inverted cask over a vigorous jet of steam for twenty minutes, then swill out when cool.

ii   Mix two fluid ounces of domestic bleach with twelve pints of water, and pour into the cask. Roll frequently during the next three hours, empty, wash vigorously, pour in a little of the sterilization solution given for jars, roll, drain and swill several times with clean water.

When a cask is emptied, wash and sterilize before storage.

Other Equipment

Sterilize as for glass jars.

Chapter 2

The principles of Wine-Making

Wine can be made from a great variety of fruits, vegetables and grain, either individually or in combination, and include such unlikely ingredients as rose petals, birch sap, spruce bark and treacle.

All wine is made on the same principle, that a 'must' is prepared, either by squeezing juice from the ingredients, or making an infusion of them. This must be then fermented with yeast, left to stand until fermentation ceases, 'racked off' without disturbing the sediment, bottled, and left to mature.

The preparation of the must, the type and amount of yeast used, and the length of time of standing are individual to their particular recipes, but the actual processes are standard, no matter what type of wine you are making.

Fermentation is a natural process, and there are natural yeasts which can, and do, ferment fruit. Over-ripe fruit on the tree will start to ferment, as will sweetened stewed fruit left in a warm place. This natural fermentation is slow and unsteady, subject to cessation when the temperature sinks below or rises above that at which the yeast can comfortably survive and increase.

In the natural process of turning must into wine, wild yeasts convert the sugar in the fruit into alcohol and carbon dioxide until the alcoholic content is about 4%, at which the wild yeast dies, and fermentation ceases.

But natural processes do not stop here, because acetic bacteria (vinegar germs) attack the wine as soon as fermentation ceases and, left to itself, the wine would soon become vinegar. This is, in fact, how vinegar is made, often unintentionally. Air-borne moulds can also spoil wine, and it is these moulds and bacteria that make it necessary to have an air-lock.

Many books on home wine-making talk about the 'illnesses' of wine, but they are seldom more than contamination due to the want of very simple precautions in excluding air, and in cleaning and sterilizing equipment.

All fruit and many vegetables contain an amount of natural sugar, and this is converted into alcohol by the action of yeast. Natural yeasts die, as we mentioned earlier, when the alcohol content reaches about 4%, therefore special yeasts are used which raise the alcoholic content to about 14%. And since the yeast converts *sugar* into alcohol, more sugar is added. The amount of unconverted sugar left after fermentation has ceased will determine whether your wine will be sweet or dry. If there is no unconverted sugar, your wine will be very dry indeed. Because the amount of natural sugar varies from fruit to fruit, there is no 'rule-of-thumb' as to the amount of sugar that should be used. Often you must follow a recipe to the letter at your first making, so that you can judge how much sugar you should add or subtract subsequently to have the wine exactly to your taste. Suiting your own palate is always a matter of experimentation.

All ingredients for wine-making, especially fruit, should be sound, and at the peak of ripeness, except in the case of apples and pears, when windfalls can be used. Fruits designated in the trade as 'jam fruit' should be used for jam, and not for wine.

To prolong the process of fermentation, and therefore to increase the alcoholic content beyond that produced by wild yeasts, cultivated yeasts are added to the must. Special wine yeasts can be bought from Boots, and Heath & Heather, and although bakers' and brewers' yeasts can be used, wine yeasts are so easy to buy now, and improve the flavour and bouquet of your wine to such a degree, that it is a pity not to use them.

Wine yeasts are available in different varieties, according to the type of wine you want to make, but newcomers to wine-making usually find the all-purpose dried wine yeasts better, because a knowledge of the different types of wine produced by different fruits come best with experience. Wine yeasts are more tolerant of alcohol, and may yield an alcoholic strength of up to 18%.

Wine yeasts are slower and quieter workers, too, and do not make the hissing and frothing produced by the vigorous fermentation of bakers' and brewers' yeasts. This is all to the good, as wine is the better for a long, slow fermentation. (Less messy, too.) If proper air-locks are fitted to your fermenting jar, the must is quite safe from the acetic bacteria, even during the longer fermentation.

It is not advisable to delay the *start* of fermentation, because the must is always vulnerable, so a yeast 'starter' can be prepared three or four days before you start wine making. A starter is simply a small amount of yeast already activated, introduced into the must as soon as possible, to start immediate fermentation.

To make a starter, take a freshly sterilized bottle of about quarter pint size, and fill it three parts full with water in which a dessert-spoonful of sugar has been dissolved. Add a yeast tablet, and plug the bottle-neck with cotton wool, so that wild yeasts and bacteria cannot contaminate the mixture.

Shake the bottle gently once or twice a day. As the yeast becomes active, the mixture will become cloudy.

CHAPTER 3

Racking, Fining and Bottling

Racking

This is the process of taking off the fermented wine (making sure that all fermentation has ceased), and pouring it into a storage vessel.

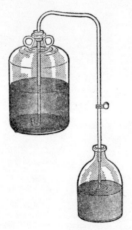

If you have a cask or aspirator jar, with a tap

near the bottom, this is simply a case of drawing the wine off carefully, as the sediment will be lying on the bottom, below the tap, and will not be disturbed.

Otherwise, syphon off the clear wine carefully, without disturbing the sediment. A length of clean tubing, plastic or rubber, $\frac{1}{4}$ inch in diameter, will do the job nicely.

Although the wine is not very nice at this stage, and may be tart (but not, we hope, vinegary, as this will show that it has been contaminated by acetic bacteria), it is as well to taste it to see if it is going to be sweet enough for your taste. If not, add a solution of 3 lb. sugar to a gallon of water. Dilute as little as possible, within the limits of compatability of taste, because heavily diluted wine is always insipid. Re-ferment to avoid dilution of alcoholic content.

Cork the jar, and wax the outside of it well, or, if using a cask, drive home the bung. Store in a cool place for at least six months, or according to the particular recipe.

Fining

This is simply another term for clearing. Many wines will become crystal clear a few weeks after fermentation has ceased, but some need to be treated with clearing agents, or they will remain cloudy.

The temporary cloudiness seen in the storage jar is caused by dead yeast cells, which will, in a short time, sink to the bottom of the jar, and are left behind when the wine is racked off.

Other materials can cause cloudiness, and if they are not removed, the wine will never clear, either in the jar, or in bottles, however long it is stored. The most common cause of clouded wine is *pectin*, a glutinous substance found to a certain degree in all fruits. In jam-making, pectin is essential, and is often added so that certain jams may 'jell' properly. But in wine, pectin causes a permanent cloudiness, especially if the fruit juice is boiled in the preparation of the must.

Isinglass is commonly used to clear wine containing pectin. If you take $\frac{1}{8}$ ounce isinglass dissolved in a quart of slowly warmed wine, and add it to the rest of the wine in the storage jar in a circular motion, the isinglass will combine with the pectin and precipitate to the bottom of the jar. The wine should then be racked again into another storage jar.

Non-precipitating yeasts sometimes cloud wine, and can be filtered out through a thick cloth.

The presence of lactic acid bacteria will sometimes cloud the wine, giving it a silky sheen when swirled. This can be treated with three Campden tablets, crushed, to each gallon of wine.

It is also possible to clarify wine by stirring in a whisked white of one egg to every fifteen or twenty gallons of wine.

Wine flavoured with powdered spice may cloud, especially if too much spice is used. This cloudiness cannot be removed, and whole spice should always be used. Another tip: suspend the spice in a muslin bag during fermentation.

Cloudiness in bottled wine is more difficult to deal with. Yeast growth can be seen by abnormal gas pressure, haziness, and a creamy-brown deposit on the bottom of the bottle. It should be re-fermented, and *not* left in the bottles, as the action of the gas may cause them to explode.

The vinegar bacteria may infect a low alcohol wine. Long chains of bacteria can be seen in the bottled wine, and may be caused by too much air space in the bottles, faulty corking, and/or insufficient waxing of corks in bottles that are stored upright. If the wine is undrinkable, the best thing to do is to allow the vinegar process to complete, because a good vinegar is a greater asset than an undrinkable wine.

If your bottled wine suffers from growth of lactic acid bacteria (look for the silky sheen), it can be treated as for the growth of the bacteria in the storage jar, but if it is heavily infected, write the wine off to experience, because the taste will be terrible. This infection is very rare, and only occurs in wine of low alcoholic content.

Bottling

Your wine is normally ready for bottling after six months in the storage jar. As in racking, the wine is carefully drawn off to prevent any remaining sediment being disturbed. Use a sterilised tube, and sterilised bottles, which should be filled up to the beginning of the neck.

New corks should always be used, and driven right home with a corking machine or a blow from a mallet, and then are better wired into position with pre-prepared loops that encircle the bottle-neck and cover the top of the cork with two tight loops.

When hand-corking, it is a good idea to lay a piece of thin plastic-covered wire, or even a strong thread alongside the cork, so that both are inserted into the bottle neck. Once the cork is in place, draw out the thread or wire, and you will bring a small quantity of air with it, lessening the likelihood of the cork being blown out by compressed air.

There is a belief, not entirely an old wives' tale, that wine bottled at the time when the plant from which the fruit was taken is in flower, will have a natural sparkle. This particularly applies to gooseberry wine, but it does happen in a lot of cases.

Bottled wine should be stored on its side, so that the cork is kept moist. A minimum of six months should pass before you drink it, or longer, as the recipe demands. And, of course, it is the better for a quiet sojourn of two or three years before it is broached.

DRINKING GLASSES

Sherry.

Sparkling Wines.

White Wine.

Red and White Wine.

Chapter 4

Wine-Making Recipes

APRICOT WINE

While dried apricots can be used to make this excellent wine, fresh fruit is preferable, especially as dried fruit wines tend to be cloudy.

The wine is quite without parallel with fish of any kind, and makes a light quick-maturing table-wine, especially delicious when chilled before serving.

1. Take 6 lb. fresh apricots, stone them, and steep the fruit in a gallon of hot water until it is soft.
2. Strain through a cloth, and add 4 lb. sugar and a teaspoonful of dried yeast.
3. Rack after fermentation ceases, and store for six months before bottling.

Using Dried Apricots
1. Soak 4 lb. dried fruit in a gallon of water for twelve hours, the cut up small and

simmer in boiling water for fifteen
minutes.

(Do not overcook, or the wine will
certainly be cloudy).

Proceed as above.

BALM WINE

In the beginning of summer before the plants
have become coarse, pick the tender shoots of
the balm, an aromatic plant, wash them in a
colander, wrap them in a dry cloth to dry off as
much moisture as possible, then bruise them
with a wood presser. Some people claim that
the leaves should not be washed, but though a
slight amount of the flavour may be lost by
doing so, we prefer the loss to using dusty and
dirty leaves.

Before preparing the balm, boil some water,
allowing 2½ lb. of sugar to each gallon. As
soon as the sugared water has cooled down,
but not become cold, put the bruised balm in
—add 1 slice of toast and ½ oz. yeast, also the
juice and rind of a lemon, 1 lb. raisins. Cover
and leave for eight days, then strain twice—
place in a cask. Press in the bung—leave the
barrel in the cellar for six weeks, then decant
into bottles. Put a lump of sugar into each
bottle before fixing the cork. Do not drink the
wine until it is six months old.

Many people prefer to leave balm wine in the cask until it is required; it's just a matter of fancy, which method is followed.

BEETROOT WINE

Though beetroots can be obtained during the greater part of the year, this wine should be made in the Autumn. First take a dozen fair-sized beetroots of full red colour and boil them with the skins on. Then when tender peel and slice them, but keep all the water they were boiled in and strain it. Next take about 6 pints sloes, or when these cannot be obtained substitute damsons, put them in 3 pints of water and mash them as much as possible with a wooden potato beater. Follow this by boiling the water and fruit for about half an hour.

Strain off the liquid and pour it over the sliced beetroot—the latter should not be placed in a metal receptacle. Add the beetroot water: after two days add 5 lb. of stoned raisins, and the rinds of 2 oranges. At the same time boil 6 gallons of water with 3 lb. of preserving sugar to the gallon for half an hour, and when lukewarm pour it over the first mixture. Spread 2 thick slices of toast with 2 oz. yeast and put it on the liquid. Cover and leave for ten days to ferment. Strain the liquid, put it with $\frac{1}{2}$ lb. of broken-up sugar candy into a barrel, close up the bung. At the end of the month strain the liquid again, add a trace of isinglass which has been dissolved in a little water, put in a wine-glass of brandy. Close the bung once more and leave the wine to keep for as long as possible. Decant into bottles when needed. Note that this wine has a somewhat rough flavour when less than a year old, and is delicious and mellow after the second year.

Do not try to keep beetroot wine as long as suggested unless the brandy is added.

BLACKBERRY WINE

This is a very economical wine to make, since blackberries can be had simply for the picking. Blackberry wine is rather like port in character, and is at its best, like port, as an after-dinner drink.

1. Pick your blackberries on a warm sunny day, wash them and drain them well.
2. Put them in a wide vessel (an earthenware crock or casserole will be ideal if large enough), in layers, alternated with layers of soft brown sugar and a few granules of dried yeast. Your proportions should be 8 lb. of fruit to 3 lb. of sugar. (Weigh them out before you start).
3. Mash the mixture with your hands, or with a wooden spoon, so that the juice

flows freely, cover the vessel closely, and leave for three or four days.

4. Strain through a clean cloth, pressing the pulp so that no juice is lost. If there is not enough juice to fill a storage jar, put it into clean bottles, adding two or three chopped raisins to each, and cork *lightly*.

   Note. This stage of the process is not to be confused with your final bottling. The juice is stored in bottles simply for convenience's sake, as an incompletely filled storage jar is an open invitation to contamination, and this wine contaminates rather easily.

5. When fermentation has finished, rack off carefully into clean bottles, cork tightly, and leave to mature for at least twelve months. Blackberry wine is apt to throw considerable sediment, and should be racked off very carefully. If you pour all your lees into one bottle, and allow to stand for a week, you can rack off again to prevent waste.

Serving

Remember to decant an hour or two before serving, and serve at room temperature, never chilled. Try a bottle or two for the Christmas a

40

year after bottling. A wineglassful added to your fruitcake or Christmas pudding will give a wonderful richness.

BLACKBERRY TABLE WINE

Blackberries make a fine red table wine in the claret class.

1. Clean 6 lb. blackberries, pour on 6 pints hot water, and mash fruit. Cover, leave for two days.
2. Stir in 2½ lb. sugar and a yeast starter, leaving to ferment in a warm place.
3. Rack and store for six months, and it will be ready in late summer.

BLACK CURRANT WINE

When the black currants are ripe and plumped up with juice, clean and pick from 6 to 10 quarts. Place them in a pan and crush with a wooden potato masher. Then pour over the mass an equal volume of cold water. Stir and stand in a cool place and cover over to keep out the dust.

Next day pass the contents through to strain the juice from the pulp; see the pulp is thoroughly squeezed in order to get every drop of juice. Stir in 1 lb. of sugar to each quart of the liquid—add 1 slice of toast with ½ oz. of

41

yeast spread on it. Leave to ferment fourteen days, covered. Pour the sweetened liquid into a cask—after straining it well. Plug the bung-hole lightly and stand in a mildly warm place. If stood in the kitchen, stand under the kitchen table; the ordinary cold cellar is hardly warm enough.

Quiet fermentation goes on for a long time and in this way wine clears itself—all the 'dirt,' known as sediment, falls to the bottom of the barrel.

Force the bung in tight and leave to mature for almost a year, when you should have a rich black wine. Then bottle and use.

BRANDY WINE

Purists will claim that this is a misnomer, and, of course, it is. But this is an ancient and traditional, and pretty strong wine, known from time immemorial as 'poor man's brandy'. And, in fact, it does taste very much like it.

1. Put into a vessel 1 lb. pearl barley, 1 lb. chopped raisins, 1 lb. scrubbed chopped old potatoes, the rind (not pith) and juice of one lemon, and 4 lbs. demerara sugar.

2. Pour on 1 gallon boiling water, and stir daily for 21 days, fermenting as soon as the mixture is cold with an ordinary

yeast starter, or by spreading yeast creamed with a few drops of water and a little sugar on to a slice of toast and floated downwards in the liquid. Keep the vessel sealed as tightly as possible, to avoid contamination from the air.

3. After 21 days, strain the liquid into a narrow-necked jar, or into bottles, **cork** lightly, and allow fermentation to continue until it ceases altogether.

4. Rack, bottle and store for at least a year. If left for five years, it will resemble brandy. Half a pint of brandy or whisky to each gallon of wine, added before bottling, will improve it immensely, and insure that it keeps almost indefinitely.

CHERRY WINE

Morello cherries, uneatable as dessert fruit, make the best cherry wine. They are not easy to buy, but if you should be lucky enough to find them, buy them when they are black, and not red. Other kinds of cherries can, of course, be made into wine, but Morello cherries are undoubtedly the best.

1. Stalk and rinse 6 lb. cherries, pour a gallon of hot water over them, and when cool, break the cherries with your fingers.

2. Leave covered for three to four days, then strain, add 4 lb. sugar in two lots, a yeast starter with the first lot, then the second lot a few days later.
3. Ferment in a warm place, then rack and store for nine months before bottling.

CHERRY 'BRANDY'

Once again, this is not really brandy, but an exceedingly rich cherry wine.

1. Take 2 lb. Morello cherries and prick them with a needle. Cover with 2 lb. brown sugar and steep in 2 to 3 pints old ale.
2. *Fill* a container with the mixture—an old sweet jar with a ground-glass stopper is ideal. Allow mixture to ferment naturally.
3. Store wine and fruit for a year, then strain the wine into bottles. Use the fruit for trifles, tarts etc.

CLARY WINE

This is a favourite wine in many parts of the country. Clary is a member of the sage family, and those who like sage as a flavouring will appreciate this wine. For our present purpose the blue blossoms of the clary are gathered if possible just before they show signs of deteriorating, which is generally in the late summer.

Pick a gallon of blossoms and boil 3 gallons of water in which has been placed 7 lb. of preserving sugar, and the whipped whites of 3 fresh eggs. This is a method of clearing wine. When the liquor has cooled down add the clary, as well as 1 large slice of toast spread with $\frac{1}{2}$ oz. of yeast. Cover. Stand for a week. Stir well and repeat the stirring three times a day.

At the end of the week, strain and pour the wine into a cask, leaving the bung loose. When the frothing has ceased, then the cask should be sealed down.

Four months later it is advisable to strain off the liquor and put it into bottles. Leave it for three months longer, then it is in a mellow condition for drinking.

Clary wine is essentially a country drink and those who make it often go by a recipe that has been in the family for several generations. Many of these recipes are quaint. In one case a farmer's wife told us her special secret. It was to pick a handful of flowers and drop them in the cask a month after the wine was commenced—it made all the difference, she said. Another housewife of our acquaintance would never dream of picking the blooms while the moon was on the wane. "How could the wine be worth drinking?" she asked scornfully, "if you did."

COLTSFOOT WINE

This recipe makes a delicious wine of its kind, moreover it is comparatively cheap.

Gather about half a gallon of coltsfoot blooms. They look like dandelions and are very common early in the season. Spread them out on a clean tray and place them where they will dry rapidly; turn them over occasionally.

When the flowers are ready, mix them with 1 lb. of stoneless raisins. While doing this, boil a gallon of water with 3 lb. of preserving sugar, and pour it straight from the heat on to the flowers and raisins. As soon as the liquid is almost cold, spread ½ oz. of yeast on a thick slice of toast, put it on the top—yeast side down—cover, and leave for a week to ferment.

At the end of this time strain through a muslin and put in a cask. Put the bung in loosely, until frothing or hissing has stopped, then close down firmly, and pour the liquid into bottles in the Autumn when it will be six months old. It will be in excellent condition by Christmas.

Many cooks add a little lemon or orange flavouring to the wine just before bottling and some consider that a trace of brandy is needed to bring out the full flavour.

COMFREY WINE

This is made from the comfrey plant, which grows by pond and stream and has drooping bell-shaped flowers ranging from a pale yellow to reddish purple. In this case it is the roots we want. They should be dug up early in spring. After being washed, scraped and cut into short lengths the pieces are put in a saucepan and boiled in water, allowing about 1 lb. of roots to 1 gallon of water.

When the roots are quite tender, the water in which they were boiled is poured into another pan with 1 lb. of preserving sugar to each quart of liquid.

The sweetened liquid is now put to simmer about an hour, when it is left to cool down. As soon as it is no more then slightly warm, put it in a bowl—add 1 thick slice of toast spread with $\frac{1}{2}$ oz. of yeast. Cover and let ferment fourteen days. Then strain—stand over night and in the morning pour the clear off and put into a cask.

Then close up the cask and bottle in six or nine months' time. The wine is then ready for drinking.

COWSLIP WINE

In the spring, pick the cowslip flowers, without any stalks, sufficient to make 4 quarts.

Then boil 8 lb. of sugar in 2 gallons of water for thirty minutes. As scum arises take it off with a wooden spoon. Then pour this sweetened liquor into a tub and when cold drop in the flower heads. Let them drown—also squeeze in the juice of 2 lemons. Stir this half a dozen times for two days, then strain through muslin and store it in a cask.

At the end of a month, bottle the liquid, dropping 1 lump of sugar into each bottle.

John Evelyn's recipe for cowslip wine has been often quoted. Here it is:

"For every gallon of water take 2 lb. of sugar, boil it one hour and set to cool. Next spread a good brown toast on both sides with yeast but before using it beat some syrup of citron with it—1½ oz. of citron to every gallon of liquor. Then put in the toast while still hot to assist the fermentation, which will take two days. Cast on the cowslip flowers a little bruis'd but not much stamp'd in the quantity of ½ bushel to 2 gallons, 4 lemons flick'd with the rinds and all. Lastly one bottle of white or Rhenish wine and then after two days turn it up into a sweet cask."

DAMSON WINE

1. Take 6 to 8 lb. dry, firm, unbroken damsons, and remove stalks. Crush fruit

and pour on 1 gallon boiling water. Cover at once, and leave for three to four days, stirring once or twice with a wooden spoon.

2. Strain must and weigh out sugar in the proportion of 3½ lb. to a gallon of must.
3. Add 2 lb. sugar and a little yeast, adding the rest of the sugar during fermentation.
4. When fermentation is finished, rack the wine, and store for a year before bottling.

This is a port-type wine, and especially delicious when a little is added to gravy for serving with roast meat. A good table wine can be made if a gallon of hot water is poured over 4 lb. damsons and 3 lb. sugar, and the must fermented in the usual way.

DANDELION WINE

It is not everyone who cares for dandelion wine—it is most like whisky. It is believed to have a bitter flavour. However, it has certain medicinal properties, being useful for liverish subjects.

Gather a quantity of dandelion flowers and pull off sufficient petals to fill a gallon measure —or complete heads can be used.

Put the petals in a bowl, pour 6 quarts of boiling water on them, add 3 sliced lemons and 3 sliced oranges. Cover and leave three days, then strain through a muslin.

To the liquor put 5 lb. of preserving sugar, a lump of bruised ginger, 1 thick slice of toast spread with $\frac{1}{2}$ oz. of yeast. When the mixture has cooled down, add to it the toast on which $\frac{1}{2}$ oz. of yeast has been spread; cover and stand four days.

Finally strain the mixture and store in a cask for three or four months, then run it into bottles for use as required.

DATE WINE

This is another dessert wine, with the added advantage that it can be made at any time of the year, because dried dates are always available.

1. Chop and boil slowly 4 lb. dates with $\frac{1}{2}$ lb. demerara sugar in a gallon of water for half an hour. Leave in a few date stones.
2. Cool, strain, and add the rind and juice of four lemons. Mix in yeast, rack and store for six months before bottling.

ELDERBERRY WINE

A slightly dry rich dessert wine, and a sovereign remedy for a cold.

1. Gather elderberries in the late autumn when they are black and beginning to droop. Strip the berries from the stalks, and pick over, as any little bits of stalk will give a bitter flavour.
2. Break up a few pieces of root ginger and, with one or two whole cloves, add to 4 lb. berries. Simmer in a gallon of water for $\frac{3}{4}$ hour.
3. Cool, strain, add 1 lb. chopped raisins, the rind and juice of a lemon, and 2 lb. of sugar with your yeast starter, and 4 half-pounds of sugar at intervals of 10 to 14 days, to prolong fermentation.
4. Keep fermentation going far as long as possible in a warm place, then rack and store for 8 to 9 months before bottling.

Serving

Always serve at room temperature. Chilling spoils it. Use it in Christmas puddings, and try casseroling a couple of pigeons in it. If you suffer from insomnia, add such spices as cinnamon and nutmeg (always use whole spices where possible. Ground spices tend to cloud a wine), and a pinch of cayenne. As a night-cap, it's quite unrivalled.

ELDERFLOWER WINE

At its best, this wine rivals even Chateau

d'Yquem, the best of white Bordeaux. Matured for at least two years, it is a wine you may well be very proud of.

1. Gather elderflowers on a warm sunny afternoon in late June and hurry home with them before they fade. Lay them on clean paper, then strip the petals from the stems. Exclude all green parts, leaves and stem, which would make the wine bitter.

2. To make a gallon of wine, simmer very slowly 4 pints of elderflowers and the thinly peeled rinds of 2 lemons in a gallon of water for 15 minutes. (Measure the flowers in a pint mug or glass, pressing them down firmly). Simmer in two lots if you have to.

3. Strain on to $3\frac{1}{2}$ lb. sugar and a few ounces of chopped raisins. Add juice of the two lemons, stir until sugar dissolves, cool, and add yeast.

4. Stand your storage jar in sunlight, if possible, as this stimulates fermentation, unless the sun is very hot (over 100 degrees), as this will overheat the wine.

5. Rack and store. Rack again, and add a few chopped raisins when bottling. Serve slightly chilled.

GINGER WINE

This is a grateful drink on a winter's night, and is considered a specific for indigestion.

1. Boil 2 oz. well-broken root ginger in 1 gallon of water with the thinly pared rinds of 2 lemons and 2 oranges, for half an hour. Add a good pinch of cayenne to the boiling liquid for an extra 'glow'.
2. Strain, pouring the liquid on to 3 lb. sugar, adding the juice of the lemons and oranges and a pound of chopped raisins.
3. Cool, add yeast, and ferment in the usual way, store
4. Rack and bottle. Mature for six months before drinking.

GOOSEBERRY WINE

Sparkling gooseberry wine is so much like champagne that its production was once forbidden, because dishonest innkeepers sold it to the public as the real thing.

This is an ideal Christmas table wine, because it goes so very well with poultry, especially a nice fat festive goose.

1. Choose small green *early* gooseberries for finest flavour. Clean 6 lb. of them, and pour a gallon of boiling water over

them. Leave overnight to soften, and
then break them open with your fingers.
(Other methods will break the seeds, and
give a very bitter flavour).

2. Leave for two days, then strain the pulp
   and add 3½ lb. sugar and the yeast
   starter. Ferment in a warm sunny
   position.

3. When fermentation has ceased, rack and
   store until the gooseberry bushes flower
   in the following spring.

4. Bottle, and leave at least to the following
   Christmas. The wine will be fine, dry,
   light and sparkling.

GRAPEFRUIT WINE

The wine is somewhat similar to orange
wine, described later, but it has a richer flavour
and is smoother if first-class fruit is selected.

Take 12 large grapefruits full of juice, wipe
them and cut them into thin slices, preferably
with a silver knife, then remove the pips if any.
Next pour over them 3 or 4 gallons of boiling
water, and having stirred it well cover up and
put on one side for a week—but stir once or
twice daily.

At the end of the week strain off the liquor
and put with it 4 lb. of preserving sugar for
each gallon of liquor—pour into a cask. When

all hissing is finished fit the bung tightly and leave for three months.

This is a quick maturing wine which must not be kept too long; it should be drunk before six months old. The absence of all other ingredients beyond sugar ensures a pure rich, flavour. We have tried a number of modified recipes containing other ingredients and do not consider the results quite as satisfactory, though we rather think that some may consider the flavour is slightly preferable if the peel is removed from the fruit in the recipe given here.

GRAPE WINE

Many people who think that the only proper wine is that made from grapes, are often surprised at the idea that it is quite possible to make grape wine at home. At first thought, grape wine would seem to be expensive to make, but if you have a good green-grocer, ask him to tell you when he has the small, seedless, sweet Cypriot grapes, and then ask him for the loose ones which fall off the stalks and normally cannot be sold.

1. Take 10 lb. of these grapes, and throw away any with green mould on them. (The brown skin spots don't matter). Rinse them quickly in cold water to

which a Campden tablet has been added, and remove loose stalks.

2. Drain well, and crush each grape between your fingers. Cover the vessel carefully and leave for 24 hours, then strain to extract every drop of juice. No water or sugar need be added.
3. Ferment with a little yeast in a warm place.
4. Rack and store for at least a year. Then rack and bottle, maturing for as long as you can hold out, at least 18 months, preferably for two to three years.

Note: The colouring in wine comes from the skin of the grapes, and therefore white wine as well as red can be made from black grapes. If you prefer a red wine, leave the crushed grapes in their juice for four or five days, until the must is the required colour.

LEMON WINE

Lemon wine has nothing akin to lemonade or lemon squash in flavour, but is a much more mellow and satisfying drink.

To make it obtain a dozen juicy lemons. Clean and peel them and then boil 3 gallons of water with 9 lb. of preserving sugar. If thoroughly clean rain water is obtainable it is to be preferred to ordinary tap water. Boil for three-quarters of an hour slowly and remove any scum that rises to the surface. Then turn the boiling water over the lemon rind in a bowl. When lukewarm, pour the juice of the lemons into it and place a thick slice of toast spread with 1 oz. of yeast in as well. Cover and stand to one side for one week.

Next strain the liquid and place it in a cask, with a loose bung. Fermentation will now go on, and from time to time listen to see if it is hissing.

When all frothing and hissing has quietened down, add a wine-glass of brandy and push in the bung tightly. Stand in a cool place for six months, then drain off into bottles.

Some housewives put in a pound of stoneless raisins for each gallon of water instead of the brandy. The raisins must then be split open and left with the liquor until it is bottled.

LOGANBERRIES

These are difficult to buy, although at one time they were a very popular summer fruit. But we include this recipe, which makes a very good port-type wine, for those who have loganberry bushes in their gardens, or who have loganberry-prone friends.

1. Pour a gallon of boiling water over 5 lb. loganberries and 2 lb. sugar. Stir until

      sugar dissolves, and crush berries with the back of a spoon.

2. Cool, and add yeast. Ferment for two days, and then strain onto another 2 lb. sugar, pressing the pulp to extract the last drop of juice. Ferment again, adding $\frac{1}{4}$ lb. sugar each week for four consecutive weeks.

3. When fermentation has finished, rack and store for six months, then rack again, bottle and keep for six months before broaching.

MARIGOLD WINE

Towards the end of July or early August gather 2 gallons of marigold flowers—not merely the petals but the heads without any stalk. See they are free of ants and other creatures.

Then boil 8 lb. of sugar and 1 lb. of honey in 3 gallons of water for an hour. When the water has cooled to lukewarm, put in a thick slice of toast spread with 1 oz. of yeast, and drop in a few of the marigolds having previously bruised them. Stand and cover over for a few days, and each day, throw some more of the marigolds in. At the end of five days all the marigolds should be thrown in, and then 2 lemons, sliced thinly, put in as well.

Leave all these ingredients for three days more. Strain and put in a cask, adding 1 pint of any white wine. As soon as fermentation is complete fit the bung in tightly, and about a year later strain the liquor and put it into bottles. It is then mellow enough for drinking.

Recipes for marigold wine vary considerably. In some cases the flowers are bruised and then boiled with the sugar, honey and water; in others, the list of ingredients includes 4 or 5 beaten egg whites. Many of them substitute brandy for white wine and others stipulate sherry. The recipe quoted here in full is, however, a very popular one which may be thoroughly recommended.

MARROW RUM

This is a traditional Norfolk recipe, and although this is of course not rum, any more then the 'brandy' in previous recipes was actually brandy, it carries a tremendous kick, and should be treated with great respect.

1. Get a beautiful, big, straight marrow, cut a two inch slice off the top, and scoop out all the seeds.
2. Fill the resulting space with demerara sugar packed as tight as you can. Dissolve a half teaspoon of yeast in a tablespoon of tepid water, and pour it on the sugar.

3. Replace the end of the marrow, and seal the join with adhesive tape. Wipe the outside of the marrow carefully and cover it with a muslin bag, tying it at the neck. Suspend it over a jug, and exclude air by placing the whole thing, marrow and jug, in a plastic bag.
4. Hang the whole thing up on a hook, and within a few days, juice will start to drip down into the jug. And by 'juice', we mean Jungle Juice!

Geographical Note

In Australia, pawpaws are used instead of marrows. Traditional instructions include a warning as to the correct method of broaching this particular keg. Lie flat on your back under your fermenting fruit, and bore upwards with a gimlet, so that the juice runs down into your mouth. Lying down saves you the pain and trouble of falling over at the first taste—and the Aussies are dedicated and hardened drinkers!

MEAD

A traditional English drink made from honey, which is coming back into fashion after a lapse of several hundreds of years. It is a fine dessert wine, and contrary to expectation, not over-sweet.

1. Bring 5 lb. honey to the boil with a gallon of water, and simmer for half an hour, skimming as necessary.
2. Cool, add the juice of a lemon, and yeast. Ferment as usual racking and storing, and then racking and bottling.

METHEGLIN

This is simply spiced mead and a small quantity of ginger, cloves, cinnamon etc., can be added to the fermented wine before storage.

A light mead table wine can be made with 2 lb. honey to a gallon of water. Maturing quickly, it can be drunk six months after bottling.

MIXED FRUIT WINE

Make a selection of soft fruits including any of the following: red currants, gooseberries, strawberries, cherries, raspberries, apricots, cherry plums, and a limited quantity of black currants, rhubarb and raisins. You can even include left-over rice pudding, crusts of bread, mashed potato and clean peapods. Or not.

1. Steep 6—8 lb. of the mixture in a gallon of water for three days, strain on to $3\frac{1}{2}$ lb. sugar, and ferment in the usual way.

2.   Rack and store. Rack again, bottle and leave for six months. It will be ready by New Year, and will be a surprisingly pleasant table wine.

MULBERRY WINE

When well-made and properly matured, this wine has a delicious flavour that is quite its own. Gather 4 lb. of mulberries in a sound condition—i.e. they must not be so soft that when collected they lose their shape and fall into a mass; nor, of course, should they be hard and under-ripe as they will then be deficient in juice.

Pick over the mulberries and pour 2 gallons of boiling water on them. Crush the berries and make them into pulp; stand on one side and cover over.

Next day strain through a muslin and put in 3 lb. of preserving sugar to every gallon of liquor. Add $\frac{1}{2}$ oz. of root ginger and a clove or two. Boil all this slowly for about an hour, skimming the scum from the surface as it rises. When the liquor has had time to cool down to lukewarm, stir in 1 oz. of yeast. Stand to ferment for fourteen days, then strain and add a wine-glass of brandy. Put in a cask and close up the bung tightly. In about nine months' time the cask should be opened and the wine poured into bottles. It is then in excellent condition for drinking.

Note that many people think it necessary to pour in $\frac{1}{2}$ oz. of dissolved isinglass just before the bung is fixed in order to clarify the wine. When this is done, the isinglass should be added without agitating the wine and so as to cover the surface.

ORANGE WINE

Make in January from Seville oranges, and you'll have a fine apertif of delightful golden colour, to drink on its own, or with gin, to add to trifles, or to drink, chilled, with pork or with duck.

1. Peel a dozen Seville oranges, removing every scrap of pith, and keep the peelings. Squeeze the oranges to remove all the juice, and add the juice to the peelings. Add a gallon of boiling water, cover closely and leave for a few days, stirring occasionally.

2. Strain off the liquid, and add $3\frac{1}{2}$ lb. demerara sugar. When the sugar has dissolved, add a yeast starter, and ferment in a warm place. Or, to delay fermentation, add part of the sugar with the starter, and the rest in small quantities over a period which could be as long as

3—4 months, making sure that fermentation does not stop at any time. Some wines are better for slow fermentation, and this is one of them.
3. Rack and store for at least six months, rack and bottle, and keep at least until Christmas.

Note. If your greengrocer has over-ripe Seville oranges he can't sell, you can use them for this wine, as the sugar content is higher. Be warned. Always make sure that no pith gets into the must, as it will ruin the wine. Drink chilled.

PARSNIP WINE

'Mock Sherry,' as this wine is sometimes called, is probably the finest wine that can be made at home, when the cost is taken into consideration. Although parsnips can be obtained all the year round, it is far the best plan to make this wine only when the roots are new and young. Large coarse roots will merely provide a rank-tasting beverage. Clean and peel 6 lb. of parsnips and cut them into short pieces. Then boil them in a gallon of water until they are quite soft. Have no lid on the saucepan during the cooking, as the flavour is then improved.

Pour off the liquid and make it up to a

gallon, if short, by adding hot water. Then put in 3 lb. of preserving sugar. Boil again for forty minutes and then allow the liquor to cool down.

When luke-warm put in it a thick slice of bread spread with ½ oz. of yeast. Leave to stand covered for a fortnight, stirring daily.

Next strain and pour into a cask, but do not fix down the bung until all hissing has ceased. Then close down securely.

Put the cask on one side for at least six months and then bottle.

PEAPOD WINE

This is a kind of bonus wine, because it can be made out of virtual rubbish, that is if you still buy peas in the pod, and not out of the Supermarket freezer.

1. Slowly boil 5 lb. peapods in a gallon of water until cooked—i.e., until they are fork tender, not mushy.
2. Strain off the liquid on to 3 lb. sugar, and stir until sugar dissolves.
3. Cool. Add the juice of 2 lemons and yeast starter, and rack and store after fermentation ceases. Bottle after six months storage, broach the following Easter, and drink with fish, poultry and/or salad.

PEAR WINE

You can use hard green pears for this, so it's a good wine to make if you have a pear tree in the garden, and get plenty of wind-falls. They make a nice light table wine.

1. Slice 8 lb. pears *quickly*, so that they don't have time to brown off, as this affects the flavour, and increases the likelihood of contamination by the vinegar bacillus. Pour a gallon of boiling water into the vessel, and slice the pears into it.
2. Cover closely, and stir every day for a week, or until the pulp is soft. Strain through a cloth, and add 3 lbs. sugar, a handful of cut raisins and some yeast.
3. Ferment as usual, store for six months, and the wine is ready for drinking very soon after bottling. Serve chilled.

PINEAPPLE WINE

Boil 1 gallon of water with 4 lb. of preserving sugar for three-quarters of an hour and remove any scum that rises to the surface.

When the sweetened liquor has cooled down, squeeze the juice out of 3 fully ripe pineapples and pour it into the liquor, also put in a thick slice of toast spread with $\frac{1}{2}$ oz. of yeast. The pineapple should be cut into slices and bruised in an earthenware dish before adding to the liquor.

Leave the mixture for six days, then take out the toast and strain. Pour the liquid into the cask with a loose bung. Fermentation will go on and when the hissing stops add a wine-glass of brandy. Some prefer to use sherry. Push in the bung tightly and stand the cask in a cool place for six months and then drain off into bottles.

PLUM WINE

Almost any type of plum yields excellent wine, but the best are Victorias, and the small dark bush plums. Victorias make a light amber wine, and the bush plums a fine red wine. They both tend to be sweet rather than dry, and are best served at room temperature.

1. Pour a gallon of boiling water over 6 lb. fruit and 2 lb. sugar, the fruit having been washed and stalked. Break up the fruit, and stir until the sugar is dissolved.
2. Cool. Add yeast and ferment for 4 to 5 days. Strain, and add a further pound of sugar.
3. When fermentation finishes, rack, store etc., as usual.

QUINCE WINE

Take 2 dozen quinces and peel them thinly—
then grate the flesh or chop it up small. Place
this pulp in 1 gallon of water and boil for
thirty minutes.

That done, squeeze the liquor through muslin
and allow it to fall on 3 lb. of preserving sugar
in a bowl—add the juice of 2 lemons. When
luke-warm, add a slice of toast spread with
½ oz. of yeast. Cover and leave for four days,
then take out the toast and pour the liquor into
a cask, but do not tighten up the bung until
fermentation ceases—which should be about
a week. Bottling should not be done until
the wine is seven or eight months old, but to
wait a year is better. This is a slow maturing
wine.

RAISIN WINE

Raisins, which are simply dried grapes, yield
a beautiful golden wine. This wine can be made
at any time of the year.

1. Chop 6 lb. raisins and add the rind and
   juice of a lemon, and 1 lb. demerara
   sugar. Pour on a gallon of boiling water,
   and when cool add a yeast starter.
2. Ferment, and proceed as usual. Mature
   for 18 months at least.

Note: If you make this wine in June, try adding a handful of elder flowers, to impart a beautiful bouquet not unlike that of muscatel. Try serving with a shortbread biscuit for 'elevenses'. This was once very much the fashion, and old customs are always pleasant to revive. This is a rich wine, and therefore should be served at room temperature.

RASPBERRY WINE

Of all the fruit wines, this probably retains the flavour of the fruit most strongly. Because of the cost of raspberries, we include this recipe primarily for people who have raspberry canes in their gardens.

1. Gather 6 lb. firm dry fruit, on a hot day, when the juice is loosened. Remove the stalks, and any bad fruit. Place them in a vessel, and crush them with your hands, then pour over a gallon of boiling water.

2. Cover, and leave for two to three days, then strain and add $3\frac{1}{2}$ lbs. sugar.

3. Mix in yeast, and ferment. Then proceed the usual way, adding $\frac{1}{2}$ lb. raisins on storing. Store for six months before bottling.

RED OR WHITE CURRANT WINE

This wine has quite a different flavour from that made with blackcurrants—of course it may not only be made with red or white currants—but also with a mixture of both. In our own opinion, however, if a mixture is decided on, the proportion of red should be—at least twice that of white currants, and frankly we look upon white currants by themselves as a trifle insipid.

Take 5 quarts of sound, plump currants, and, if home picked, they should be gathered on a dry day. Take off the stalks, put them in a bowl, and squeeze out the juice with a wooden spoon. Boil 10 quarts of water and 10 lb. of sugar together for ten minutes and pour over the currants. Cover and keep for one week; stir occasionally.

Strain and squeeze every drop of juice out. Strain again. Fermentation will take place, but will continue more quietly. Place the liquor in a cask, and leave the bung loose until the hissing has ceased. Then most wine-makers pour in a glass of sherry and close up the bung.

In six months' time the wine should be in admirable condition for bottling.

Note that raspberries may be used instead of part of the currants, and the same applies to loganberries. The only thing is to keep the total quantity of fruit the same as suggested above. In our opinion, raspberries help to give a smoother taste, which is an advantage.

RICE WINE

Rice wine, (saki), is one of the most popular alcoholic drinks in the Far East, where it is given flavour and fragrance by the addition of lime or lemon flowers, or spices. The rice used is wholemeal (unhusked), and this is best, if you can buy any, although the commoner polished rice can be used, and makes a very strong wine.

1. Crush 3 lb. rice with a rolling pin, or pass it through a mincer. Add 3 lb. sugar and 1 lb raisins, the thinly pared rind and the juice of a lemon, and a gallon of boiling water. Add small quantities of spice, the florets of a couple of heads of elder flower, or the petals of a dozen common orange marigolds, if you like. Any of these add flavour and fragrance.

2. Stir the mixture, and when cool, add yeast. Cover and keep in a warm place for a week to ten days, stirring every day.

3. Strain through a clean cloth, and continue fermentation until activity ceases. Rack and store for 6 to 9 months before bottling.

This makes a fairly strong table wine to serve at room temperature, and which may have to be sweetened slightly to suit your taste before decanting. If you prefer it dry, chill before serving, and you will find it very good with shellfish.

RHUBARB WINE

Take 10 lb. of rhubarb when the sticks are at their best. The very early varieties have insufficient flavour and the coarse, thick sticks are too rank. Mid-season sticks coated with reddish skin are required. Wipe the rhubarb with a cloth and cut it into dice but avoid skinning it. Put in a large vessel, pour on 2 gallons of boiling water, cover and leave fourteen days then strain off the liquor—add 8 lb. of sugar to the liquor, stir until the sugar is dissolved. Add a sliced lemon and a sliced orange and 1 oz. of root ginger. Cover and stand fourteen days. Strain, pour into a cask, fix the bung tightly. In six months' time pour out the wine through a strainer into bottles—it is then ready for use.

ROSE PETAL WINE

This is looked on by many people as a curiosity, and it is, indeed, an unusual wine, capturing as it does both the taste and fragrance of roses.

1. Collect the fallen petals of dark red fragrant roses until you have two quarts when pressed down in the measures. (The petals will keep for a week, and if you can't collect two quarts, make a smaller quantity). Pour on a quart of hot water, and macerate the petals thoroughly with a wooden spoon. Steep until cool, strain, and then repeat the process with another 2 pints of water. Press the petals firmly to extract all the essence.

2. Mix the rose water with 4 pints of water in which 3 lb. sugar have been slowly boiled for 20 minutes. Add yeast and ferment in the usual way. Rack and mature the wine for a year, so that the exquisite bouquet can develop.

   Serve at room temperature.

ROWANBERRY WINE

Rowanberries are the bright red berries of the Mountain Ash, and they can be made into a sound little dessert wine.

1. Gather the berries when ripe and dry, and steep them in an equal quantity of boiling water, e.g., a quart of berries to a quart of water. Add a piece of root ginger, and the juice of a lemon, and stir daily for 10 days, macerating the berries to release the essences.
2. Strain on to 1 lb. sugar for each quart of must, add yeast and ferment in a warm place.
3. When fermentation has finished, rack and store for 6 months, then bottle and keep for a further 3 months.

SAGE WINE

The amount of sage required for this wine is a point on which no two housewives agree, and it's not unusual to find one who will use eight times the quantity considered correct by another. Here the amount specified may be looked upon as a minimum, which is what we believe is most satisfactory.

Boil 2 gallons of water and when it has cooled down pour it over 9 lb. of stoneless raisins which have been cut open, also add $\frac{1}{2}$ gallon of sage leaves cleaned and finely chopped.

Add 4 lb. of sugar, stir well, then leave covered for a week. Next strain the whole of it through muslin, squeeze all juice out and strain it again.

Put it in a cask, leave the bung loose until the hissing is quiet, then close down tightly. A week later remove the bung and pour in a glass of brandy and close up once more. Six months later the wine may be bottled; put the corks in loosely for three days, then make firm.

We do not consider that the wine is fit until it has been in bottle for six months; even then it will decidedly improve up to one year.

SHERRY

A good recipe for making home-brewed sherry is the following:

Put 5 gallons of water in a pan with 12 lb. of sugar and boil for half an hour, removing the scum as it rises to the surface. When the sweetened liquor has cooled down mix with one gallon of fermenting infusion of malt, which can be obtained from a local brewer or made by fermenting ordinary malt purchased at the Corn Chandlers.

Leave for four days, add 5 lb. of chopped stoneless raisins, 2 oz. of dissolved isinglass and 2 lb. broken sugar candy. Cover and leave a fortnight to ferment.

Strain well and put the liquor in a cask.

When the hissing has ceased put in $\frac{1}{2}$ pint brandy and fit the bung tightly. It is usual to empty the cask of its contents after about six months to strain the liquor and clean out the cask—then to replace the wine in it and close up the bung.

Bottling should be done when the wine is a year old.

Many recipes suggest considerably more brandy than we have done and the quantity here may be regarded as the minimum.

SLOE WINE

Pick a gallon of sloes when they are ripe, which is usually in late September, and roll them in a damp cloth to clean them. Place them in a bowl, pour a gallon of boiling water over, put in 5 lb. of preserving sugar, cover and stand for fourteen days, stirring often. Strain, and put the liquor in a cask.

Fermentation will now proceed slowly and while it continues the bung should be loose. On ceasing to hiss, pour in a wine-glass of brandy and $\frac{1}{2}$ oz. of dissolved isinglass, then tighten up the bung.

Sloe wine takes a long time to mature, so that it should not be bottled under a year— even when bottled it improves when kept six months longer.

STRAWBERRY WINE

Take 8 lb. of luscious strawberries, pick them over and then squeeze them; use a wooden spoon for the purpose. Pour on to them 1 gallon of cold water, stir well and leave for three days. Squeeze and strain through a muslin—strain again, add 3½ lb. of sugar, stir and cover. Leave a week—then strain into a cask, put the bung in lightly. The ideal condition is to have the cask full at the outset.

In ten days fermentation should be complete. Then pour in ½ pint whisky and fix the bung tightly.

This wine matures fairly rapidly—it may be bottled after six or seven weeks and drunk almost at once.

SUMMER WINE

Gather a quantity of soft fruits such as strawberries, raspberries, redcurrants or whatever happens to be available. Mix them up as you like, as the quantities of each do not matter. This it will be seen is an admirable way of making some delicious wine when there is not sufficient of any fruit to warrant a particular brew.

Clean the fruit as each kind demands, put the whole in a bowl and crush it thoroughly. As the juice runs out, pour it into a suitable

77

vessel and go on crushing the pulp until little remains with any goodness in it.

Now put ½ lb. of preserving sugar with every pint of juice and stir until thoroughly dissolved. Cover the vessel with a cloth and leave for three days. At the end of this time strain the liquor, put twice as much white wine with it as there is liquor, and fill into bottles.

The wine may be drunk on the expiration of ten days.

TOMATO WINE

The tomato is now known to be a valuable food, being rich in vitamin property. Thus this wine may be offered as one that is not only tasty and refreshing but nourishing as well. To make it, procure a quantity of good juicy tomatoes, wipe them clean then mash them with a wooden spoon. Place the mash in sieve and allow the juice to trickle through—this, it may be said, is a slow process. When all the juice has been collected sweeten with white sugar (¾ lb. to each quart), put in a pinch of salt, stir well and cover up.

Leave for the fermentation to proceed, but skim off the froth on the surface occasionally. In the course of time, the liquor will be quite clear and if properly strained, free of sediment. Turn into bottles, well corked, and store for three months at least.

WHITE WINE

This a cheap and easily made wine. Boil 3 gallons of water with 9 lbs. of preserving sugar for twenty minutes. Skim the liquor, then put it in a tub and when lukewarm add 3 lb. of raisins chopped fine. Add 2 thick slices of toast, each spread with ½ oz. of yeast. Cover and stand one week.

Strain, put in a cask with ¼ oz. of dissolved isinglass, and if desired ½ pint of brandy. Tighten up the bung when hissing ceases.

In eight to twelve months' time the wine will be ready for bottling and drinking.

WHORTLEBERRY WINE (Blaeberries)

This is a delicious wine that should be made by anyone who has the opportunity of going out and picking a suffecnt quantity of whortle-berries.

Pick a gallon of the berries and then go through them to remove stalks, leaves etc. Put them in a pan and squeeze them with a wooden spoon. Then pour a gallon of boiling water over them—bring to the boil and simmer ten minutes, strain. Add 4 lb. of preserving sugar, stir thoroughly. When lukewarm add a thick slice of bread (no yeast). Cover and stand one week—then strain and put in a cask.

Insert the bung lightly for fourteen days, then fix the bung securely. In a year the wine should be in a rich condition and it may then be bottled and drunk.

Many recipes suggest a little nutmeg should be grated and put in the cask after fermentation has ceased. In our opion the wine is finer without it.

HOW TO MAKE LIQUEURS

It sometimes happens that a batch of wine turns out to be a little undistinguished, often due to the quality of the fruit used. This undistinguished wine can take on a tremendous distinction if used as the basis of a fruit liqueur.

1. Take a couple of bottles of white wine, and pour over 8 large ripe peaches, stoned and sliced, or 2 lb. stoned halved fresh apricots, or a large pineapple peeled and diced. Add 1 lb. sugar and a few grains of wheat, cover, stand in a warm place to ferment steadily. After fermentation, store for 9 months, syphon off and then bottle.

2. If using red wine, take blackcurrants, blackberries, loganberries or raspberries. Blackcurrants should be topped and tailed, and used in the quantity of 1 lb.

to two bottles of wine and 1 lb. demerara sugar, because they have a very strong flavour.

When using other berries, wash and stalk them, and use 2 lb. for each two bottles of wine.

Chapter 5

Ales, Beers, Cordials, Etc.

This section is devoted to several pleasing beverages that are of a miscellaneous character. They all serve the same purpose, however, so much as they enable the housewive to produce wholesome drinks that may be stored and kept until required.

Most of the following are easier to make than the wines described under the previous heading and all are cheap to produce except when the recipe has brandy as one of the ingredients.

BLACKCURRANT GIN

Sloe gin is known to everybody as an acceptable drink, but those who have tried blackcurrant gin often prefer it.

Bruise 2 quarts of picked and cleaned blackcurrants in a stone jar, add 3 lb. of dark demerara sugar and pour over 3 quarts of gin.

Stir well and cover over. Take off the cover occasionally and stir afresh.

At the end of three months strain off the liquor and pour into bottles. The longer it is kept, within reason, the better. (If too sweet for your taste, add some more gin.)

CHERRY BRANDY

There are several recipes for making this cordial. The simplest is to gather some cherries —Morellos and black ones in equal quantities, and to fill a bottle three-quarters full with them. Then the bottle is filled with brandy and corked tightly. A month is the minimum time that must elapse before the wine is drunk.

It is highly important that the cherries should be sound and not over-ripe.

Another recipe is to select the cherries as above and to put them in a bottle with crushed sugar candy, allowing 4 oz. of candy to each pound of fruit. Then brandy is poured in to fill the bottle, while the cherries and sugar should only fill it to the extent of three-quarters.

Many people do not pull the stalks from the cherries but cut them so as to leave half the length. Such cherries can then be served up in cocktails and other refreshers, and the stalk permits them to be conveniently consumed.

FRUIT CORDIAL

Gather a quantity of summer fruits of the raspberry and redcurrant kind and let them be sound and juicy. Put them in a stone jar and stand the jar in boiling water. Very soon the skins will burst and the juice will accumulate at the bottom of the jar.

Strain the contents, then add half as much brandy as there is juice. Put in an ounce of broken-up sugar candy for each pint of liquor.

Allow this to stand covered over for one week, then strain and bottle. The cordial may be drunk after two months.

If not to your taste add a sugar lump to each bottle. Give it time to marry, say three weeks, then taste and add again if necessary.

(This method may be applied to almost all the soft fruits of summer—if it is desired to deal with one kind at a time. In the case of loganberries, the quantity of sugar candy should at least be doubled).

GINGER ALE

Take 3 quarts of water, 1 lb. of loaf sugar, 1 teaspoonful of tartaric acid, 1 teaspoonful of ginger essence, 1 oz. of caramel colouring and a pinch of cayenne pepper.

First boil the water, including the sugar, and

let it continue to boil for five minutes. Then put the tartaric acid in a large jug and pour the sweetened water over it; allow it to cool and add the ginger essence, the caramel and a pinch of cayenne. Stir well and the drink is ready for the table as soon as it is cold. It will keep well, however, if bottled.

GINGER BEER

Take 1 gallon of water, add 1½ lb. of white sugar, 1 oz. of root ginger, 1 oz. of cream of tartar, ½ oz. of yeast and 1 lemon.

Boil the sugar and the ginger with 2 quarts of the water—then put the cream of tartar into a large jug, and pour 2 quarts of cold water on to it. When dissolved add the boiled water. Stir well, then squeeze in the juice of the lemon and mix the yeast to a cream with a little sugar before adding to the whole.

Leave until next day, then skim off the yeast and the drink is ready for consumption. When desired for storing, it is better to follow the recipe given for Ginger Wine.

HOP ALE

If undecided as to whether to make Hop Ale or Hop Beer, it is highly probable that the beer will be preferred.

For Hop Ale, take 4 oz. dried hops, 2 oz. dandelion root and if obtainable 2 oz. of gentian root, and boil them in 6 gallons of water for 2½ hours. As soon as the liquid is lukewarm strain it—stir in 6 lb. of dark brown sugar and 2 oz. of yeast spread on a slice of toast. Stir well and cover.

Next day squeeze out the bread and strain the liquid. Stand some hours and pour off the top to leave the sediment behind in the bottom. Put into a cask, fit the bung tightly, and stand on one side for a few days when it will be fit for drinking.

HOP BEER

Take 4 oz. dried hops, 2 lb. bran and 6 lb. sugar and boil them for 2½ hours in 6 gallons of water. As soon as the liquid is lukewarm mix with it 2 oz. of yeast, stir well, and cover over.

Leave for four days, then lift off the scum with a wooden spoon and follow this by straining the liquor. Place in a cask and fit the bung securely.

In a week the beer may be drawn from the wood and drunk, or if preferred it may be bottled and used as required, when corks should not be driven in for twenty-four hours.

MALT ALE

Put the following ingredients in a pan containing 5 gallons of cold water: (*a*) 2½ gallons of malt, (*b*) 2 oz. of dried hops, (*c*) 2 oz. of whole ginger. Then boil them for two hours. Strain.

As soon as the hot liquid has cooled to lukewarm add 5 lb. of crushed sugar candy. Stir until this has dissolved. Add ½ lb. of brewers yeast. Leave two days, then take off the scum and bottle the clear liquid.

NETTLE BEER

This is a very pleasant drink and one that may be taken in the spring as a good blood purifier. Pick about 1 gallon of nettle leaves, selecting the young, light green shoots at the tips of the stems. Wash them in a colander and shake dry. Also purchase 1½ lb. of malt at the Corn Chandler and obtain an ounce of dried hops as well as ½ oz. of root ginger. Put all these together and boil them in 1 gallon of water, continuing to keep them on the boil for twenty minutes. Stir during the process.

Then pour the liquid on to 1 lb. of loaf sugar, and when cooled to luke-warm put in 2 ozs. of sarsaparilla and ½ oz. of yeast. Stand the mixture on one side and when it is hissing

violently owing to fermentation put it into
bottles.

It is ready for drinking almost at once.

ORANGE BRANDY

Peel 6 Seville oranges of fair size, break the
peel into pieces and pour a quart of good
brandy over it. Cover up securely and set on
one side for a week. If a stone jar is used place
a parchment covering over the opening as is
done with jam jars. At the end of the week
take a quart of cold water, put into it 1 lb. of
loaf sugar and boil down until the liquor is no
more than a pint.

When this sweetened liquor is cold add it to
the brandy, strain the mixture and put into
bottles.

This cordial may be drunk when a month
old.

PEACH BRANDY

Cut up a quantity of ripe peaches that, however, are not over-ripe; or better still, break
them into fragments with the handle of a
teaspoon. The great thing is not to use any
steel implement for the work.

Put the flesh into a screw-stopped pre-
serving jar, half filling it. Then sift in $\frac{1}{4}$ lb. of
sugar candy broken small and fill up with good

French brandy. Screw down very tightly and stand the jar aside in a cool, dark cupboard.

At the end of a month or six weeks pour off the liquor into bottles and cork up with a film of sealing wax as an additional precaution against the syrup turning.

PINEAPPLE BRANDY

This is an unusual cordial, but in our opinion it is a very appropriate drink to take when eating nuts.

Peel a pineapple, cut it into slices and weigh them. Then pack them in a stone jar, sprinkling crushed loaf sugar between the slices. The total weight of the sugar used in this way should be about half the weight of the flesh of the pineapple, and when fruit and sugar are put in, the jar should be about half full.

Now pour brandy in, bring the level up so that the jar is three-quarters full, stand on one side for four or five weeks, then pour out the liquor—strain it, and put it into bottles.

SACK

A beverage mentioned by Shakespeare and even earlier writers.

It is made by putting a few fennel roots previously washed clean and three or four sprays of rue leaves in 2 gallons of water and then boiling for forty-five minutes. Do not be too generous with the fennel, in fact we rather feel that it might well be left out altogether.

Next pour the liquid through a muslin to strain it and add 5 lb. of honey. Once more put the ingredients to the boil and keep them going for close on two hours. If froth arises, as it probably will, skim it off.

When the mixture has become cold, turn it into a cask, bung it up tightly and bottle at the end of a year.

Note the quantity of honey may be increased if a sweeter and richer flavour is desired.

Note also that whenever possible the quantity of wine should be regulated so that the cask is practically full at the outset.

SLOE GIN

Take ½ lb. of ripe sloes and roll them in a damp cloth to clean them. Then obtain ¼ lb. of loaf sugar and a bottle of gin. Put all the ingredients into a stone jar large enough and seal up; occasionally it advisable to shake the jar and even to stir the contents.

At the end of three months—longer if possible—strain off the liquor, and pour it into bottles.

If the sloes are pricked before putting them into the gin, the time taken for liquor to mature is curtailed.

TREACLE BEER

This drink has many favourites. Make it in the following manner: Turn 1 lb. of treacle into a large pan and pour 2 gallons of boiling water over it. Stir well and when lukewarm add half a pint of yeast. (2 oz. will do, spread on a thick slice of bread.) Cover the pan and two days later remove the surface scum. Strain and bottle.

VINEGARS

BLACK CURRANT VINEGAR.—Place some ripe black currants in a stew pan, add a very small quantity of water, sufficient to keep the fruit from burning, put over a mild heat until the juice flows from the currants. Then strain through muslin, add a little less than 1 lb. of loaf sugar to each pint of warm juice and when cold put in a tablespoon of brandy. Finally double the bulk of the liquor by adding white vinegar. Bottle and cork.

PINEAPPLE VINEGAR.—Peel and cut up a pineapple of average size. Put the slices in a pan with a pint of white vinegar, leave for a week, then mash up the flesh of the pineapple to release as much juice as possible. Strain through a muslin. Boil the juice and vinegar for twenty minutes with loaf sugar—using ½ lb. to each pint of liquor. Bottle and cork.

RASPBERRY VINEGAR.—Put some raspberries in a pan, mash them with a wooden spoon and pour on ½ pint of white vinegar for each pound of fruit. Leave for a week, covered up, but stir occasionally. At the end of the time strain and put 1 lb. of loaf sugar to each pint of liquor, then simmer gently for a quarter of an hour. Bottle and cork.

STRAWBERRY VINEGAR.—Put a convenient quantity of strawberries in a pan, mash them and just cover them with white vinegar. Leave for a day, then strain through muslin and add 1 lb. of loaf sugar to each pint of liquor. Simmer for half an hour and bottle when cold.

List of Suppliers

Birmingham
Boots the Chemist,
City Centre House
and other branches.

City Health Centre,
10 Union Street,
Birmingham, 2.

T.A.S.C.O. Chemists Ltd.,
816 Bristol Road,
Selly Oak, Birmingham, 29.

Bristol
Boots the Chemist,
Broadmead, Bristol
and other branches.

Heath & Heather,
19 Broadweir, Bristol.

Redland H.F.S.,
29 Zetland Road,
Bristol, 6.

Cardiff
Boots the Chemist,
806/808 Newport Road,
Rumney, Cardiff.

Health Food Stores,
39 Wellfield Road,
Roath Park, Cardiff.

Davis Bros. (W. & S.) Ltd.,
77 Pontanna Street,
Cathedral Road, Cardiff.

Edinburgh
Boots the Chemist,
Princes Street,
and other branches.

Bristol Health Food Stores,
2 Bristol Place, Edinburgh.

Exeter
Boots the Chemist,
The High Street
and other branches.

Southern Health Foods Ltd.
23 North Street, Exeter.

Southern Health Foods Ltd.
1 Odean Buildings,
Sidwell Street, Exeter.

Glasgow
Boots the Chemist,
Union Street
and other branches.

Health Food Stores,
11 Dundas Place,
Glasgow, C.1.

Logan Health Food Stores,
10 Dixon Avenue,
Glasgow, S.2.

Newhealth,
25 Buckingham Terrace,
Glasgow, W.2.

S.H.S. Ltd.,
203 Buchanan Street,
Glasgow, C.1.

Leeds
Boots the Chemist,
Briggate
and other branches.

Curtis H.F.S. Ltd.,
4 Fish Street, Leeds.

C. M. Stead,
41 Merrion Street, Leeds, 2.

West Yorkshire H.F.S.Ltd.,
20 Eastgate, Leeds.

Curtis H.F.S. Ltd.,
144 Roundhay Road,
Leeds, 8.

Clapham's Ltd.,
Vicar Lane, Leeds, 1.

Leicester
Boots the Chemist,
2/4 Haymarket, Leicester
and other branches.

Leicester Health Food
Centre,
2-3 Charles Street,
Leicester. (Mail Orders)

Liverpool
Boots the Chemist,
Church Street
and other branches.

Cooper's Stores,
Church Street, Liverpool.

Atherton's,
15 Oswald Street,
Liverpool, 13.

Sefton Park Health Food
Stores,
8 Lawrence Road,
Liverpool, 15.
(Postal Service Tel: Sefton
Park 2059)

London
Messrs. Gamages,
Holborn, E.C.1.

The Lima Shop,
59 Station Road,
Winchmore Hill, N.21.

M. D. Brody,
Chemists,
138 High Road,
Willesden, N.W. 10.

Healthiways Health Food
Store,
Cheseman's Ltd.,
Lewisham, S.E.13.

Harrods,
Knightsbridge, S.W.1.

N. Cole,
4 Granville Arcade,
Coldharbour Lane,
Brixton, S.W.9.

Heath & Heather,
5a Leigham Court Road,
Streatham, S.W.16.

Heath & Heather,
19 Goodge Street,
London, W.1.

Heath & Heather,
232 King Street,
London, W.6.

Manchester
Boots the Chemist,
Cross Street
and other branches.

Health Food Store,
307 London Road,
Hazel Grove, Manchester.

Henry Woodhead & Co.,
16 Cathedral Street,
Manchester, 4.

Newcastle
Boots the Chemist,
Northumberland Street
and other branches.

Blake's Medical Stores Ltd.,
10 Haymarket,
Newcastle upon Tyne.

Nottingham
Boots the Chemist,
Pelham Street
and other branches.

Savoy Health Food Store,
16 Exchange Walk,
Nottingham.
(Postal Service Tel: 44693)

Sheffield
Boots the Chemist,
High Street
and other branches.

Health Food Store,
174 Norfolk Street,
Sheffield.

"Sunshine Shops",
Orchard Street, Sheffield.

Swansea
Boots the Chemist,
1 Oxford Street, Swansea
and other branches.

H. J. Llewellyn,
31 Alexandra Road,
Swansea.

Waynes Stores Ltd.,
41-43 Uplands Crescent,
Uplands, Swansea.

Mumbles Healthfayre,
622 Mumbles Road,
South End, Mumbles,
Swansea.

Index